To access online media visit:
www.halleonard.com/mylibrary

Enter code:

4772-7562-4153-0512

Praise for *The Art and Heart of Drum Circles*

"Christine Stevens can guide groups to the secret world of the rhythmic arts."
—Mickey Hart, Grateful Dead

"There is a growing belief that every human being is inherently musical. This book provides the path to music making that the world has been waiting for."
—Joe Lamond, President/CEO,
NAMM, National Association of Music Merchants

"Christine Stevens can introduce you to the magic, fun, and healing power of drumming. I recommend it."
—Dr. Andrew Weil, MD, Author of *Healthy Aging*

"An exceptional compendium of insights certain to make any drum circle a success, this book is a MUST read!"
—Barry Bittman, MD, CEO Mind-Body Wellness Center

"Christine Stevens brings together the energy of her drum circle leadership and her background in wellness to give us a very helpful book."
—Dr. Will Schmid, MENC Past President and
author, *World Music Drumming*

"A very thoughtful and sensitive approach to drum circles to make music making successful for EVERYONE!"
—Lynn Kleiner, ORFF instructor/educator,
founder, Music Rhapsody, producer of Babies Make Music series

"Christine Stevens inspires the creative and playful spirit in all of us, no matter how deeply it is/has been tucked away."
—Kelly Burgos,
Music Cares, Grammy Foundation

"An easy hands-on guide to creating successful music-making experiences for all ages."
—Barbara Reuer, PhD,
Resounding Joy, MusicWorx,
Past President of American Music Therapy Association (AMTA)

"Christine is a master at building energy and unifying audiences through rhythm."
—T. Harv Eker,
Author of #1 *New York Times* Bestseller
Secrets of the Millionaire Mind

The ART and HEART
of Drum Circles

The ART and HEART of Drum Circles

Second Edition

CHRISTINE STEVENS

Hal Leonard Books
An Imprint of Hal Leonard LLC

Second edition published in 2017 by Hal Leonard Books
An Imprint of Hal Leonard LLC
7777 West Blue Mound Road
Milwaukee, WI 53213

Trade Book Division Editorial Offices
33 Plymouth Street, Montclair, NJ 07042

First edition published in 2003

Printed in the United States of America

Library of Congress Control Number of the first edition: 2003103735

ISBN: 978-1-5400-0218-1

www.halleonardbooks.com

To Remo Belli, 1927–2016

Contents

Foreword

by Arthur Hull

In the beginning, each of the pioneers of the modern drum circle facilitation movement, Jimmi Two Feathers, Sadonia Cahill, Barry Bernstein, Ubaka Hill, Bob Bloom, Arthur Hull etc., were rediscovering the basic universal principles of how a rhythm-based event worked.

Like the story of seven blind people feeling different parts of the elephant, each one thought that they were alone in their discovering, uncovering, and recovering this ancient art form. Each had their own perceptions of the "blinding flash of the obvious." Is it a rope, a tree trunk, a wall, or a snake?

In our quest, we also started to discover the other drum circle pioneers. We then realized that our perceptions were individual windows that looked into the infinite possibilities of what rhythm-based events could become. When we combined and compared, these "windows of perceptions", they became individual facets in the jewel that is the modern drum circle movement.

Back when drum circles were considered a fad or a phenomenon, this diamond was just forming. It had only a few facets and lots of possibilities. Now twenty years later I find myself standing in the middle of a well-established grassroots, non-professional hand-drumming movement, where a lot of those possibilities have manifested. The jewel is taking shape. This has happened because all of the emerging drum circle facilitators are coming together to share their discoveries and points of view. In this process, they are creating a community of drum circle facilitators.

I now also find myself standing next to Christine Stevens, who, in the last few years, has been a major networker in our growing drum circle community. Through her position as Director of Health and Wellness at Remo, she has been able to connect the many different facilitator facets together from many parts of the globe. She has empowered the drum circle community with her knowledge, spirit, and enthusiasm.

I am glad to see Christine add her facet to the diamond by writing this book. It is a major contribution to our knowledge of the what, the why, and the how of rhythm event facilitation. The title of this book reveals the "window of perception" she has to offer us. It is a fresh point of view that, as a drum circle facilitator, I can support and use. As more of the next generation facilitators add their facets to the diamond, the future of facilitated rhythm-based events is beginning to take shape. With this book, Christine Stevens not only shows us the future, but she helps us get there.

My thanks go out to her for this wonderful contribution.

Arthur Hull, Village Music Circles, author, *Drum Circle Spirit*. Visit his website at www.drumcircle.com.

Acknowledgments

Remo and Ami Belli, without whom the drum circle movement would not be where it is today. They are my teachers, as we experiment in the weekly drum circles in North Hollywood, California at the Remo Recreational Music Center.

Jean O'Sullivan, a great editor and writer, musician and artist, who kindly reviewed this manuscript on many occasions and created a dialogue that facilitated the best way to present the information.

Brad Smith, who approached me at a NAMM show amidst the noise of the percussion booths and invited me to work on this project for Hal Leonard.

Barry Bittman, MD, neurologist, researcher, author, producer, and photographer, who has been an inspirational mentor and co-facilitator of the HealthRHYTHMS training programs.

Karl Bruhn, the father of the music making and wellness movement, an incredible mentor, great clarinet player, and inspirational human being, whose commitment to the vision of recreational music making is undaunted and clear.

Arthur Hull, an incredible inspiration, the man who first opened my eyes to the concept of a community drum circle and supported my involvement in the music industry every step of the way.

Connor Sauer, who has been in the background with a wealth of knowledge, through her experience facilitating drum circles for women's groups for over twenty years. Her wisdom is woven throughout this book.

Chalo Eduardo, who has taught me the joy and the fun of samba rhythms in drum circles.

John Fitzgerald, my co-facilitator on an incredible three-country tour of Asia, working with many groups.

To everyone I've ever drummed with…thank you for sharing your heart, your rhythm, and your love of music and humanity.

Introduction

This book will cover ways that empower you to begin drum circles for your community, workplace, school, music store, family, church, yoga center, YMCA, spa, and wherever else you'd like to get one started. Written in two sections, it reflects the simplicity of the elements of a drum circle; the music and the people (the art and the heart). Drum circle facilitation is a direct reflection of this duality including both your musical ability and the way you support the possibility of human transformation while showing you care.

While materials alone can never teach what experience gives you, we all have something both to teach and learn. Your ongoing teachers will be…

The people who come to your drum circles
Solicit their feedback. Learn what they liked and didn't like.

The facilitation community
Join the drum circle yahoo group of over 2,000 drum circle facilitators by sending an email to drumcircles-subscribe@yahoogroups.com. You can also join the DCFG Drum Circle Facilitators Guild, http://www.dcfg.net/.

Your video camera
There is no better teacher and critic than you watching you.

Training programs
Ultimately, an experiential live training program will give you opportunities to practice and develop your skills with expert feedback.

For me, facilitation is like being part of a team of runners in a marathon that began long ago. We each carry a torch, a flame of musical spirit that began in ancient times when people gathered in community to drum and dance to uplift their spirit and celebrate life. As each facilitator joins the team, we reach out and light a new torch, as we remember the origins of the first flame. As the drum circle movement continues to ignite many people's hearts and spirit, there is a growing need for music-making opportunities and facilitators to lead them.

Pick up the torch. Join the race.

The ART and HEART
of Drum Circles

I

The ART of Drum Circles

Wisdom of the Ancients

Where and when did drum circles begin? Who invented this practice of drumming together in a circle? What was the ancient purpose of drum circles?

Although we can never definitively answer these questions, we can theorize, and many scholars have and do. One thing is for sure; most cultures have drummed for rituals, celebrations, and ceremonies. Drum circles seem to tap into the primal need to share and support one another through one of the simplest and most beautiful ways to connect without words; music.

Trend Alert

At one time considered a hippie grassroots thing on beaches and in parks, drum circles are now taking place at the likes of Toyota Corporate headquarters and the World Federation Banking Conference. From executives to spiritual seekers, young children to well elderly, this practice of group drumming is much more than a fad. Get ready for a real wave of music making that has the potential to change our culture and restore the power of community gatherings.

Recreational Drumming

The term *recreational* is actually derived from the Latin "recreatio," which means "restoration to health" (Merriam Webster). A research study by Barry Bittman, MD, sponsored by Remo, demonstrated the power of drumming for health purposes. The study found that one hour of group drumming with normal subjects who had never drummed before, following a specific protocol called group empowerment drumming™, reversed the stress response by significantly increasing NK (Natural Killer) cells (Bittman et al. "Alternative Therapies," January, 2002). This groundbreaking study launched a new credibility for drum circles and recreational drumming as a method of stress reduction and as a preventive-health strategy. (For more information on the research and training programs, go to www.remo.com/health, and click on *Health*RHYTHMS.)

Recreational drumming provides important musical skill development, including rhythmicity, improvisation, and ensemble playing. But it also reaches far beyond musical benefits. Including stress reduction, self-expression, and community connection, the emerging philosophy of recreational music making is not about becoming a technically proficient performer. It's really about finding the music within everyone and giving drumming enthusiasts and hobbyists a way to keep making music in their lives.

Recreational Drumming Philosophy

Group drumming is not about inspiring successful drumming—
it's about inspiring successful living.

Group drumming is not about exceptional performance—
it's about exceptional support and personal expression.

Group drumming is not about teaching people to play—
it's about giving people permission to play.

Group drumming's best facilitators are not only talented musicians—
they are caring, compassionate and intuitive guides.

Group drumming is not about acquiring technique—
it's about sharing for the sake of personal empowerment.

(Used by permission, Remo Inc. copyright, 2001, *Health*RHYTHMS™ training manual, Bittman, Bruhn, and Stevens)

Drum Circle Principles

Combining an ancient practice with today's cultural need for creative expression and human connection creates a powerful alchemy all rolled into one aesthetic experience called a *drum circle*. Drum circles can vary, but most follow similar principles.

There is no audience
Everyone is part of the musical experience.

There is no rehearsal
The music does not come from reading notes on a sheet of music written in the past. It is improvised in the moment.

There is no right or wrong
The drum circle is a safe, permissive explorational environment.

There is no teacher
Instead, the drum circle is lead by a facilitator who has a dual focus; to build the musicality of the group while also building the sense of community and connection.

It is inclusive
Everyone is welcome; all ages and all levels of ability.

Spontaneity thrives
There really is no plan except the importance of supporting the music and community connection.

It's about much more than drumming
In fact, a survey at the Remo Recreational Music Center found that the highest ranked reason people attended the Tuesday night drum circles was actually to reduce stress! (50 percent) Only 35 percent reported they were there to learn how to drum.

Drum Circle Duality

I define the drum circle as *a collective container for self-expression.* There is an incredible duality within the drum circle of creative freedom and the unity found in the common pulse. It is similar in terms of the human side of the drum circle where self-expression found through improvisation is balanced by the demand and structure of following the group rhythm. This duality is lost when the drum circle becomes a music class. This book addresses this paradigm specifically, without wavering into teaching rhythms, only demonstrating and cultivating that which is already in all people.

The Science of Entrainment

Entrainment is the law of synchronization that causes two separate rhythms to naturally line up when placed near one another. Technically speaking, it is a "phase locking" or "going with" one another, creating a natural flow. In drumming, entrainment happens when two people with separate rhythms can't help but join together in a common beat. This principle was originally discovered through physics experiments in the late 1600s, where two pendulums placed next to one another, swinging at different tempos, eventually fell in sync. Because we are rhythmic in nature, the same thing happens to us. The key is letting go and not trying too hard. The only thing that can interfere with the natural property of entrainment is the mind.

Exercise: Bird Watching

Watch a flock of geese flying in formation up in the sky. They flap their wings in perfect synchronicity, a rhythm that actually carries them 70 percent more efficiently as they entrain to the leader's dominant tempo.

Exercise: People Watching

Watch people crossing a street or walking down a sidewalk together. They unconsciously step in sync, entraining to one another's rhythm. Keep an eye out for examples of entrainment where people move together, where rhythm commands congruency and unison.

The Circle

"Drumming is essentially a social behavior. When we connect with other humans through rhythm, devoid of race, culture and prejudice, there is something pure and compelling about it. Circle drumming is very social, very human."

– Joseph Walker,
High School Principal

Circle—(*noun*) revolving about a common center. (Merriam-Webster.com)

Calling in the Circle

The artistry of the drum circle really begins before any drumbeats are heard. It begins with how you get the word out. The way you communicate about the drum circle has a huge impact on who will join and what they will expect. For posters, emphasize the great benefits of being part of a drum circle:

- Fun
- Self-expression
- Stress reduction
- Social interaction and community building
- Exercise for mind, body, and spirit
- Camaraderie and support
- Multi-generational family activity
- Develop key musical skills; such as rhythmicity, improvisation, and ensemble playing

Make sure to include key phrases like:

- Instruments provided, OR, Please bring your own drums and percussion.
- No prior musical experience necessary.
- All levels welcome.
- All ages welcome.

Enlist key pollinators in your community, people who can get the word out. Think outside the box. For a women's drum circle, send emails or flyers to the college campus women's studies program. And don't be discouraged by a low attendance the first time. When they happen regularly, drum circles have a natural tendency to grow (for more ideas, go to www.remo.com, click on "drum circles," and click on "start your own.")

Setting the Circle

Since the beginning of humankind, people have gathered in circles for an important reason. The circle creates community. There is no hierarchy. A sense of equality prevails. The circle is a container for powerful transformation, a vehicle to build up community and celebrate life.

To set up your circle, start by establishing the center. Place a drum or other marker in the middle and place chairs (preferably ones without arms) equidistant from the center. Even standing circles benefit by having a centerpiece, such as a blanket, to focus on. The center of the circle is not a "stage." It is empty, waiting to be filled by the energy of the group, the facilitator, and perhaps a few dancers along the journey. Leave space for entry paths into the circle and remember to make room for wheelchair seating. No one likes feeling cramped, so allow space between chairs for people to be comfortable and not feel "forced" into more intimacy than they're willing to gamble. If you have a drum circle of thirty or so, you may want to have one big circle. If you are working with larger groups, concentric circles help everyone hear each other's beat. Even after everyone arrives, there may be an empty chair or two. Don't be too quick to pull these chairs away. Empty chairs often represent "the ancestors." Welcome their presence into your circle and the music will soar.

Chairs set up at Remo Recreational Music Center

Coping with non-circular settings

Ovals and squares—Invite people to switch places throughout the drum circle to create more mixing. Position the bass drums and bells closest to center point. Fill in the longer spaces with people sitting on floor.

Stages, churches, and performance venues—You may begin on stage, but gradually move to the center of the floor and ask everyone to turn towards you. You can create an immediate sense of circle. If you must be on stage, invite some brave souls to join you.

Rooms with large pillars—Make sure everyone can see your cues. Don't place chairs behind pillars in the "blind spot" of the facilitator.

Creating Your Team

Many more people than the facilitator alone compose the successful drum circle. You will need to create an inner circle to support the outer drum circle experience. Utilize your human resources to amass a team for the following roles:

Job	Description
Set Up	Arranging drums and chairs to help set up the circle.
Greeters	Welcoming people as they enter. It helps to see a smiling face first thing when you arrive. They also remind people to remove their rings before drumming.
Designated Drum Distributors (DDDs)	Roving around the circle making sure everyone has an accessible instrument to play. They also look for people who need assistance with their drum, need mallets, or want to try a new instrument.
Rhythm Allies	People you can count on who can support the groove or play bass drum or bells.
Tear Down	People who help collect instruments and put the equipment away.

***Remember to thank and acknowledge your drum circle team.
That's an element of the art of facilitating that should never go unheard.

The Instruments

"Drums are an immediate tool of engagement because everyone can do it."

—Participant at Planetree Conference drum circle

Instrument—(*noun*) a means whereby something is achieved, performed, or furthered. A device used to produce music. (Merriam-Webster.com)

The real instruments that make up the drum circle are the *people*. The drums become their voices. The drum offers an immediate portal into musical expression, a quick-start experience with an instant learning curve. The rhythm of the drum has been beating inside us since before we were born. People are amazed they can do it!

Sometimes people bring their own drums and percussion instruments. However, if you are providing the drums, consider a few possible ways to distribute them.

Arranging the drums

- Have the drums beautifully arranged in the center, allowing people to take what they want.

- Have the drums pre-set on chairs in a variety fashion. This is good for starting the drum circle quickly with a larger group of people all arriving at the same time.

- Place the drums on a table near the circle near the entrance for people to choose as they arrive.

Many facilitators have their own "kit" of drums. This may include both purchased drums and found sounds they have handcrafted. As you are building up your drum kit, look for drums and percussion instruments that are...

- Lightweight
- Portable
- Durable
- Weatherproof
- Simply tuned or pre-tuned
- Low maintenance
- Kid-proof
- Nesting

For these reasons, the Remo world percussion instruments are excellent for recreational and drum circle purposes. I've been using the same thirty paddle drums for the past seven years and they still sound great!

If you don't have enough instruments for everyone, be resourceful. Remember that there are both internal and external instruments that can be used in the drum circle...like the voice and body percussion sounds.

Remo Versa drums
http://remo.com/products/product/versa-drum-pack/
http://remo.com/products/product/drum-circle-drum-pack/

UpBeat Drum Circles Sound Shape 3 Pack
http://www.ubdrumcircles.com/products_drumtrio.html

The Acoustic Landscape

It's important to offer a wide landscape of acoustic sounds to support the personal exploration and discovery of the best instrument for each person. Referred to as "timbre groups," (Hull, 1998) each instrument group makes a unique contribution to the drum circle through different acoustic roles.

Although the list of world percussion instruments is as vast as the size of the globe (I'm always finding a new, sometimes obscure instrument from some faraway country), here is a good beginning list of the multicultural mosaic of the instruments within the drum circle and their roles.

Timbre Group	Role	Instrument Origin
Bass Drums	This is your musical co-facilitator. Facilitate entrainment. Low end. Key role.	Surdo—Brazilian Dundun—West African Gathering/Pow Wow Drum— Native American Bombo—Peruvian Nesting Djun-Djun— American/Arthurian Taiko—Asian Kid's Gathering Drum— Kids/American
Hand Drums	Fill in the groove.	Djembe—West African Doumbek—Middle Eastern Congas and Bongos— Latin American Tubano—Remo invention Frame Drums—Multicultural
Mallet Drums	Support the pulse.	Buffalo Drum—Native American Sound Shapes—American Frame Drums—Multicultural
Pitched Instruments	Great for soloing and creating a melody.	Cuica—Brazilian Slit Drum—African among other cultures Boomwhackers—Whacky Music Joia Tubes—Joia Percussion Sound Shapes—Remo
Shakers	Help fill in subdivision of time. Offer shy people an immediate sense of safety.	Rattles—Native American, African Maracas—South American, Cuban, Brazilian Shakers—Multicultural

Timbre Group	Role	Instrument Origin
Wood Sounds	Staccato percussion sound. Great time keeper.	Claves—Latin American Puili Sticks—Hawaiian Lumi and rhythm sticks— Multicultural Guiro (gourd scraper)—Latin, Caribbean
Bells	Loud. They cut through. Assign carefully. Can be melodically pitched.	Cowbells—Multicultural Agogo (2-toned Bell)—Brazilian African and Tibetan Bells
Tambourines	Very easy to play. Good on the backbeat. Played often in churches.	Tambourines—Italian, European, American Riqq—Egyptian Pandeiro—Brazilian
Ambient Instruments	Give color to composition. Great for people struggling to stay on the beat.	Ocean Drum—Remo Spring Drum—Remo/Trilok Gurtu invention Thunder Tube—Remo/Robert Fishbone invention Rain Stick—Central and South American, American Indian Chimes/Wind Chimes—Tibetan, Multicultural

Exercise: Two by Two

Like Noah's Ark, I prefer to include at least two of every instrument so no one has a feeling that they are alone. Especially when it comes to the bass drums, which carry the great responsibility of providing the foundation for the groove. Everyone deserves a drum mate for an immediate sense of bonding. This creates partners in the sea of percussion sounds.

Location, Location, Location

There are three key rules in choosing a home. These same three rules apply to positioning the drums in the drum circle. Place the bass drums in the inner circle, across from one another and equidistant, so that both sides of the drum circle benefit from feeling and hearing the low end. It also helps to have the cowbell or samba bells similarly placed to provide the equal high end to the bass. (see photo on pg. 11)

Color My World

The drum circle can be as much a visual as an auditory experience. Providing colorful, fun instruments really helps people feel less intimidated and gives the drum circle a great look! Some colorful instruments include:

Sound shapes—nesting flat drums in circles or shapes that come in six colors. (www.remo.com)

Boomwhackers—pitched tubes of many different colors. (www.boomwhackers.com)

Rhythm sticks—in four colors.

Colored scarves—come in six colors. Great to get people dancing. (www.aeIDEAS.com)

Colored sticks (Hot sticks) and mallets—build your own by covering any mallet with a colorful silk swatch to create a visual extravaganza!

Fruit shakers—lemons, oranges, apples…you get it! (www.remo.com)

Sound shape drum circle at the
Remo Recreational Music Center

Exercise: Rhythm Kaleidoscope

Using Remo's Sound Shapes™ with a group of kids, you can build a rhythm kaleidoscope, and turn the common drum parade into a visual extravaganza. Use flags or scarves of matching colors to the sound shapes (red, yellow, green, blue, purple, black) and select six children to be flag carriers. Have all the children with similar colored sound shapes line up behind the child with their color flag. Begin a strong rhythm on a gathering drum in the center of the room and invite the lines to march in place. Once they have the beat, cue them (I use a samba whistle) to begin marching, weaving around one another's lines, to create a kaleidoscope of color and rhythm.

Ambient Instruments

Ambient instruments give people who feel they are rhythmically challenged or worried about "losing the beat" an immediate feeling of success. They add *acoustic color* to the drum circle song. Stopping a groove and featuring these sounds can create a break for the drummer's hands, while allowing the beauty of these instruments to be heard and recognized.

- Spring drums and Thunder tubes

- Rainsticks

- Ocean drums

- Bells

- Wind chimes

Ambient percussion instruments—ocean drum, spring drum, thunder tube

17

Bells and Whistles

How can a facilitator be heard above a crowd of loud drums? Here's where the bells and whistles come into play. Using a cowbell or a samba whistle, or playing their personal drum louder than anyone else, helps their voice be heard for musical facilitation cues. Not only should the instrument be loud, it should be unique. If you are the only one with a set of claves and you play a cue, the group will respond.

I tend to show up with a few signature facilitation tools of my own...

- Bamboo flute, fife, or penny whistle – I LOVE to put a melody over a good groove.

- Soprano saxophone.

- Samba whistle.

- Extra mallets.

Why bring extra mallets?

- For older people with more fragile hands.

- For beginners. The mallet is an easier way to start drumming.

- For loud instruments like timbales and snares that can be played softly with mallets.

- For kids—mallets really make drumming fun.

Sample Kit

Everyone's facilitation kit is different and reflects how they work with groups. I want to share my top-ten list with you here. (For more faciltiator's top-ten choices, visit remo.com/drumcircles, and click on "suggested gear.")

Racks of world percussion at Remo's Recreational Music Center (RMC)

Top Ten Instruments I couldn't live without:

1. Bass Drum (Surdo, Gathering Drum, or Tan-Tan)

2. Cowbell (handheld)

3. Rainstick

4. Nesting Drums – like frame drums and VERSA drums

5. Danceable Drums – like sound shapes or paddle drums

6. Djembes – I prefer festival djembes in all three sizes

7. Tambourines – just a few

8. Shakers – for the shy types

9. Kid-friendly items like kids' percussion drums and mallets

10. Flute – any one of a variety – Native American, fife, Penny Whistle

The Art of Facilitation

Top Shelf Photography

"Facilitation is about awakening the musical potential of creativity and play in individuals and communities."

—Andrew Belinsky, Drum Circle
Facilitator and Founder, Namastage

Facilitation—(*noun*) to make easy. (Merriam-Webster.com)

Drum Circle Facilitators

A facilitator is not a teacher. The facilitator is more like a coach, serving to inspire, direct, conduct, and lead a group of people through the discovery of the rhythm that has been waiting inside them all along. Rhythmic music comes naturally. There's no need to "teach" what everyone already "knows." Rhythm is innate. Does a baby need someone to teach them to walk? Absolutely not. But they do need support as they gradually stand on their feet and begin to take their first steps. The facilitator's job is to support the group as they play and reach out a helping hand when things get a little wobbly.

Seven Essential Skills

To represent the skills of a drum circle facilitator, our *Health*RHYTHMS™ team at Remo created a character to symbolize the key elements of a good facilitator. We named him Mick, (short for Rhyth-MICK). Mick and I have visited six different countries over the past two years, training drum circle facilitators. No matter what language is spoken, everyone seems to understand the meaning of the symbolism.

> ***Tool Belt***—essential musical and personal tools to construct and build up the circle.
>
> ***Conductor's Baton***—conducting the group through body language and clear cues.
>
> ***Flashlight***—guiding the group rather than leading them. The torch that illuminates the group's spirit.
>
> ***Big Heart***—showing that you care and caring so much that it shows.
>
> ***BIG Ears***—listening more than playing. Choosing your next move based on what you hear from the group. Listen for their ideas and feature them in the music.

> ***Coat of Many Colors***—your unique gifts for inspiring the circle. From tap dancing to playing a saxophone, facilitation comes in many colors. Make yours reflective of YOU.
>
> ***Spontaneous Steps***—being flexible, open, and in the moment. (Dancing is optional, but spontaneity isn't!)

Art by Bill Patterson

Conducting and Cueing

When asked what constitutes good conducting technique, well-known conductor Dr. Larry Livingston, former Dean of the Thornton School of Music at the University of Southern California, identified two key elements:

> ***Conviction***—a prerequisite for leadership.
>
> ***Authenticity***—command only works if the leader is authentic.

The most popular method of conducting the drum circle is using the body. But there are a variety of ways to conduct and cue the group, including:

Your voice

A whistle (à la Samba schools and marching bands)

Your drum (à la West African ensembles)

A melodic instrument

No matter what method you use, successful cues must be:

Clear—The cue must be big enough for all to see. To make sure no one is in your blind spot, rotate your body in a circle as you prepare to give your cue.

Consistent—To avoid cue confusion, use the same cue to mean the same thing throughout the drum circle.

Cool—Facilitation is a visual job. Watch yourself on video to make sure you're not doing something unconscious that is embarrassing or miscommunicates your intention.

Cues to Use

Body cues are like a rhythmical sign language that communicate your musical intention to the drum circle. Your repertoire of cues is like the eight notes of a scale. They will enable you to create infinite melodies.

1. Rumble
Hands shake to indicate a drum roll.

Rumble soft

2. Stop/Start

Countdown—"4-3-2-1- STOP" using your fingers. When starting back up, only count to two to give the proper rhythmic warning, "1-2-Ready – GO!" If you're uncomfortable counting down or up, try making a big, clear "stop-cut" (Hull, 1996). In a stop-cut, the body freezes after a motion that resembles calling someone safe on home base.

Stop

Stop

3. Keep Playing

Rolling your arms. Indicate which drummers you want to keep playing. Keep one half of the circle going before you indicate the other half to stop. That way you'll avoid unexpected silence.

Keep playing

Soft   *Getting louder*

4. Loud/Soft

Arms held up high for loud. Arms held down low for soft. (I sometimes have to put my finger over my lips and "shhhh" the group as well). Everything in between is gauged from these extremes. This cue gives the most freedom to create a dance out of your facilitation!

5. Speed up/Slow down

By showing the current pulse of the groove with your body or an instrument, and then beginning to move or play gradually faster, you can push the tempo. Slowing down is always a greater challenge!

6. Mark the Pulse or Mark an Accent

There are infinite ways to show the pulse. You can step, rock, dance, or use your arms in the center to stabilize a shaky pulse by just visually showing the underlying beat. To show an accent, an emphasis on one beat, some facilitators just air-drum a strong beat, while others do a little jump on the beat they want emphasized.

Clap the pulse

Dance the pulse

7. Sculpting, a term used by Arthur Hill (1998), refers to sectioning the circle. Be clear about who you're selecting for any one of the above cues; have them keep playing or get loud, etc. You can "cut the pie," by indicating the boundaries of the section, or come up with your own creative way. Make sure to get their agreement before you feature them. You can sculpt:

- the whole drum circle

- one section

- one instrument or timbre group

- one individual player

Sculpting shakers

Sculpting a group

Sculpting an individual player

8. Cupped Ear

This cue is my personal favorite because it reminds the group to listen to each other. Used in conjunction with pointing out a particular player or even a timbre group, this symbol encourages the group to notice their own music and balance their playing. By cupping their hand over their ear and making an inquisitive face, the facilitator mimes the importance of tuning into each other's playing, usually creating an instinctive volume down.

9. Call and Response

Pointing to yourself and then the group, miming the concept of taking rhythmical turns. I play - you play.

10. Nice Job

One of the most important cues you'll use is the "way to go" sign. A smile and a thumbs up to the whole circle communicates encouragement, confidence, and acknowledgement. Invent your own cue to say "nice job."

Grabbing the Wheel

There is a simple formula to guide you in knowing when to jump in to offer a change in the musical direction. It's like recognizing when you need to "grab the wheel." If the circle is losing control or the groove is wavering, be ready with something in your tool belt to build it back up and steer it back on the road.

There are times when facilitation is not necessary! Relax and enjoy the jam! After all, the drum circle is their circle, not yours. It's just as important to recognize when NOT to facilitate, as it is when to facilitate.

Cueing the Cue

What happens when the facilitator's cues are not clear or you don't know they're coming? The group becomes confused. There is less enjoyment and a new anxiety emerges, "What am I supposed to be doing?" Always judge your success by the look on the faces of the people at your drum circle.

Cueing the cue

To avoid confusion with your cues, always add a preparation beat on the "and" of the downbeat with the cue. Like winding up before delivering a punch, your cues need a little preparatory signal. If you think of facilitation like driving, you must put on your turning signal before you make a new musical change in direction.

Developing Your Personal Style

Just as the same instrument will sound completely different when played by two different people, no two facilitators should look the same when facilitating the drum circle. Facilitation naturally amplifies who you really are. Be creative and develop your own personal style that reflects who you are. Try this exercise to develop your own personal cues.

Exercise: Reflective Rehearsal

Stand neutral in front of a mirror with your eyes closed. Imagine that you have laryngitis and you need to tell a large group of people to STOP. Count to three and then jump into a pose. Open your eyes. Examine your pose and observe the way your body communicated. Come back to neutral.

Now think about a conductor completing a symphonic performance. Imagine the ending of the piece, right before the huge applause. Without thinking, move immediately into this pose. Examine your pose in the mirror and observe your body communication. Come back to neutral.

Now consider both these cues and test whether they are big and strong enough for an entire group to see you. Keep experimenting with a mirror, air-facilitating along with a strong-grooving rhythmical song.

AUDIO TRACK 3

Melodic Facilitation

A melody instantly creates a strong pulse and a clear rhythmic groove. I have used soprano saxophone, Irish penny flute, bamboo flutes, my singing voice, and even a Colonial fife as facilitation tools. This practice harkens back to the ancient flute/drum combination that appears in world music from many different cultures. I've even seen an excellent bagpipe player who facilitated 200 drummers in something that was akin to an Afro-Celtic recording.

Helene Barbara

Cueing while playing

The melody can be constructed to cue accents and other percussion parts
AUDIO TRACK 7. Because holding your instrument makes body cueing a
unique challenge, either cue the group with your foot or by waving your
instrument, or simply use the melody to clearly indicate what you want the
group to do.

Top Ten Tips for Melodic Facilitation

1. *Bring the volume down.* Before introducing your instrument, quiet
   the drum circle to allow the melody to be heard. This will create a
   predictable practice where the drum circle will automatically play
   softer when they see you raise your instrument.

2. *Play a well-known song.* ("Tequilla," "The Pink Panther," "Aiko
   Aiko," "Wipe Out," and anything from Herb Albert or Santana)
   This allows the drummers to play predictable solos and accents.
   This works well for seniors who have easily identifiable favorite
   tunes.

3. *Improvise an invented song.* If they are improvising, why
   shouldn't you? Try using pentatonic scales to simplify your
   choices. Invent melodies that incorporate "rhythm hits" – one-
   or two-note accents strategically placed within the melody.

4. *Use repetition.* When you invent a nice melody, keep playing it.
   Like your cues, it will become predictable and facilitate creativity.

5. *Leave space.* It's important to create dialogues with melody and rhythm.

6. *Try call and response.* You can do call and response dialogues between individuals or the whole circle with your melodic instrument. It's fun to use certain ornamentation that clearly translates into drum technique; such as trills = rumbles.

7. *Introduce a new scale.* Use an Egyptian scale: D – E♭ – F♯ - G – A – B♭ – C♯ – D and notice how the rhythm naturally changes.

8. *Do a duet.* Select one player to continue playing while everyone else gets soft. Play off their rhythm, allowing the melody to change and take a new direction from them.

9. *Take a solo.* Alternate between solo instrument and the whole group drum circle. Using A-B-A form, you can create a fun dialogue on a grand scale. For example; A-drum circle, B-saxophone solo, A-drum circle, B-saxophone plus all the tambourines, etc. This gives everyone's hands and ears a break.

10. *Mirror a drum pattern.* Amplify someone's pattern by taking their rhythm and putting your notes to create a melody.

Facilitation Disclaimer

Learning to facilitate drum circles does not make you a music therapist, even if you do drum circles for a hospital or medical setting. I don't recommend the terms "drum therapy" or "rhythm therapy" because it confuses the public and gives the impression that there is a formal course of study and professional degree in drum circles. If you want to offer drum circles to special populations or in medical settings, consider co-facilitating with a music therapist or seek additional training, such as Remo's *Health*RHYTHMS™ weekend programs, to expand your knowledge. For more information, visit www.music-therapy.org or www.remo.com/health/.

Arranging and Re-Arranging

Helene Barbara

"We come as a very young family to celebrate music and community. It is very fortifying, even if I'm just dancing around with my kids to the incredible rhythm of the drum circle."

—Jennifer Scott-Lifland, Arborist;
Noah Lifland, Furniture Designer;
Kerin and Lucia Lifland

Arrange—(*verb*) to combine so as to achieve a desired or maximum effect. (Merriam-Webster.com)

Arranging entails selecting various voices within a band or orchestra and drawing a chart of the overall map of the musical path. Arrangers are big picture thinkers, working with big tools, like an entire string section or a long melodic theme. They have a specific responsibility that is different than composing. Taking themes and creating patterns of voices, the arranger develops a thematic big picture that is balanced and aesthetically pleasing.

In drum circles, arranging refers to the way the facilitator gives form to the drum circle to achieve a desired effect. This cannot be planned. In fact, the facilitator is basically improvising on the highest level, *improvisational arranging*. In the drum circle, the players are improvising and so is the facilitator, arranging the musical and human elements within the drum jam.

Simplicity is the key. With just a single facilitation element, such as dynamics (working with loud and soft and everything in between), a facilitator can make a beautiful arrangement using repetition and variation.

Listen to arrangements in different genres of music. Orchestral forms include theme and variation, prelude and symphonic movements, adagio and allegro. Popular music forms include verse, chorus, versus, and a bridge. Sacred music forms include antiphonal, or call and response with a cantor. This will give you ideas for creative ways to use your cues in the drum circle.

Forming the Composition

The drum circle is a unique art form, requiring facilitation to support its constantly emerging song. The facilitator improvises in the moment from a repertoire of standard forms and cues.

Form	Description	Example
A-B-A	An example of A-B-A form is a verse-chorus-verse. This arrangement tool ends as it begins (see the exercise on book-ending).	The facilitator begins with bass drums only (A). Once a groove is established, they cue everyone to join (B). When it's time to end the jam, the facilitator stops everyone except the bass drums, who just play the pattern that started the piece (A).
Repetition/Ostinato	Like "looping" a phrase, a key tool in arranging is working with an "ostinato," a repeated pattern.	The facilitator has one section of the circle play a specific 4-beat pattern, while everyone else just jams. The facilitator stops them, and now begins their ostinato pattern on beat 3, while everybody jams.
Theme and Variation	This takes the ostinato one step further. Now the ostinato becomes a theme. Each time it is repeated there is a variation.	Working with dynamics, the facilitator does an 8-count volume up, followed by an 8-count volume down. After a little jam time, the facilitator has only half of the circle do the volume up/down, then the other half. Again, a little jam time, and the facilitator now has a quarter of the circle do the same thing.

Form	Description	Example
Round	Taking one phrase and starting it at different moments around the circle.	I've seen both Barry Bernstein and Lori Fithian use the familiar "Row, Row, Row Your Boat" and divide the circle into four groups. They create a round with only the rhythm of the song.
Call and Response **AUDIO TRACK 6**	One person plays back a pattern that is echoed back to them by the group.	Facilitator plays a 4-count bell pattern and indicates everyone to play it back to them.
Dialogue	A dialogue where two players or two sections speak to each other through their playing, taking turns.	Facilitator sets up pairs across the circle from each other. The first player uses their drum to ask a question, and their partner across the circle replies. This can also be done with full instrument groups dialoguing with one another.
Layering In and Layering Out	Starting with one person and adding in one at a time. Layering out is the reverse. Be careful; this can be a facilitator's concentration game.	The facilitator chooses just one bass drum player to start. That player then nods at someone else who joins in. This practice continues until everyone is jamming. It ends in the reverse. (It's easier to do this around the circle one-by-one.)
Sculpting	Having one person or a group keep playing while everyone else stops.	The facilitator indicates for just the tambourines to keep playing. Then the facilitatior counts down 4-3-2-1 and stops the rest of the circle to listen to the tambourines. The facilitator cues or counts the rest of the circle back in.
Nature	Using instruments to imitate nature like sound-effects.	Making it rain. The facilitator has everyone rub their drums to create wind. Then switch to tiny water drops by tapping the drums. Then switch to big rain by using full hands on the drums. Then add thunder (cymbals, thunder tube, bass drum booms), and end by reversing these steps.
Story	Using a story to form the composition of the improvisation.	The facilitator orchestrates a story. I like to use the story of Morgon-Kara, as told by Joseph Campbill in "Drumming at the Edge of Magic," (Hart, 1990).

Exercise: Book-Ending
At your next drum circle, try beginning with a clear musical idea, and ending with the same thing. This is called "book-ending," a Hollywood term derived from the idea of book-ends that hold everything together, and only indicates the beginning and the ending. This arrangement tool gives the drumming a circular feeling.

Arrangement Tools
The drum circle duality; the people and the music make up the basic tools for arrangements.

Musical Elements:
    Dynamics

    Instrument groups (timbre)

    Tempo

    Meter

    Silence

Human Elements:
    Breath

    Body percussion

    Vocal percussion

    Dividing by age or gender groups

    Grouping by themes – all the people born in January, all the people wearing toenail polish

Key Principles of Arranging

Law of Opposites—If you want people to play soft, cue them to play loud first. If you're having trouble getting a group to do some facilitation cue, try the opposite one first. It's like arranging in reverse psychology. If you want someone's attention, "whisper."

Law of Reversal—Any facilitation you do, you can do backwards. If you do a volume up very gradually, you can come back the next time the circle calls you and do a volume down. This doubles your repertoire immediately.

Law of Contrast—There's nothing like drama. In all good drama, there's a villain and a hero. In the drum circle, we create the drama with contrast. One half does a fast rumble, while the other half goes slowly. A loud bass drum rumble is followed by a shaker rumble, creating an awareness of the wide acoustic parameters of the drum circle.

Law of Repetition—Any repeated phrase can only stay stagnant for so long before it needs to grow and change. Although repetition is key in aesthetics, be aware of where boredom dominates, and take the arrangement challenge to keep building it up.

Law of Structure—Structure provides flexibility. There is a myth that creative freedom means "no structure." It would be much harder if someone just told you to play "whatever you want" without any form or foundation. Don't be afraid to put structure into the drum circle song. It actually helps people get more creative.

Law of Pacing—Creative ideas come fast - implementing them takes time. Go slowly and make every step clear as you arrange the drum circle song. Give each element time to sync into the groove before moving into your next arrangement idea.

Exercise: Expanding Your Horizons

Try limiting yourself to one musical cue for thirty minutes of a drum circle. For example, just use dynamics. In fact, any one of the facilitation cues can fill up thirty minutes. Your creative improvisational ability will expand as you experiment with arrangement ideas to fill the time. Your own desire to keep the music alive and growing will demand more originality and creativity.

Soundscapes

The one bias you probably have if you are a drummer or musician is that success is measured by staying on the beat. What if there was no "beat?" What if you removed the entire concept of making the drum circle happen within a driving rhythm? Can you still make music?

Welcome to a new drum circle art form that does not require a beat. Instead, it emphasizes texture and timbre, contrast and color. More like sonic poetry, this arrangement form is called *soundscapes*. Just as a landscape is the visually expansive panorama, a *soundscape* is the acoustic plane that captures the mood, effect, and subtle aspects of sound. **AUDIO TRACK 5**

Based upon aesthetic properties, such as repetition and contrast, the facilitator becomes a painter, using a palette of sounds from both the instruments and the participants, to create music.

Exercise: Contrast Dialogues

Try composing a *soundscape* by having people with contrasting instruments sitting across the circle from one another create non-rhythmical dialogues. In the beginning, you have to cue each of them, however, once the pattern is established, they will continue the dialogue and come to some resolution on their own. You can use a rumble with the whole group in between introducing new dialogue teams.

New Facilitiation Cues

Sound	Facilitation Cue
Rumbles (drum roll)	Hands shake from thumb to pinky
Drum brush	Rub hand in air in circular motion
Sound splashes	Flick with hand
Single booms	Point with strong arm—always give upbeat cue
Drum rap (on shell)	Mime tapping hands on outside of drum

Acoustic Palette

Vocal sounds	Breathing, yawning, coughing, yelling, screaming, cheering, scatting, laughing, growling, chanting, speaking
Body percussion	Snap, clap, rub, tap knees, pat head, belly drum. (Check out Body Beat™ a card game using body percussion,www.ubdrumcircles.com.)
Drum sounds	Booms, rumbles, splashes, brushes, scratches, shell tapping
Ambient and Percussion sounds	Ambient-sounding instruments (rain stick, ocean drum, thunder tube, spring drum)

For Example

The drum circle groove has been going strong all night. Now you bring it to a giant stop-cut ending; 4-3-2-1-STOP. Silence. You cue the rainstick and everyone stops in amazement to hear the beauty of this subtle sound. You layer in everyone else rubbing their drums to create a wind sound. You give a large strong cue to the bass drums for three hits, followed by one sustained cue for all the bells. What a beautiful contrast. And none of it is "in time." You continue this dialogue between bass and bells until you eventually don't need to cue it anymore. They are naturally following the dialogue pattern, and even speeding up their responses to one another. Eventually, you bring in the drums with a loud rumble and a strong stop. Once again, you feature just the rainstick (book-ending), and then it's 1-2- back to the groove....

Teaching without Teaching

"The magic, energy, and connections that happen in the drum circle effect my students in ways that they cannot get with paper, pencil, or computer. It is with great passion that I facilitate joyful and successful drum circles which transfer into positive self-esteem."
—Abbie Ehorn, School Music Teacher

Teach—(*verb*) to instruct by precept, example, or experience. (Merriam-Webster.com)

It requires real mastery to demonstrate basic drumming technique during the drum circle without putting anyone into performance anxiety. A key approach I learned at the Village Music Circles' Hawaii Facilitation Training, developed by Arthur Hill, is the importance of putting people at ease while secretly developing their drum skills, without scaring people into "student crisis mode." (Hull, 1998). It's always more fun to learn through playing a game than being "in class."

Basic technique is crucial in preventing unnecessary injuries and expanding the creative repertoire of the drum circle participants. I think of this like yoga, where the correct "Posture" is a key element.

Proper technique

A Pound of Prevention

We often hear that the drum circle is better than a pill because it has no negative side effects. But if a facilitator does not inform the group of how to play the drums, you may later hear about injuries and bruises that could have been avoided. To avoid reports of problems the next day, and a bunch of angry phone calls, it's important to cover a few ground rules:

- Briefly stretch hands, wrists, and arms.

- Reminder to relax shoulders.

- Remove rings and bracelets. (Bring bandages to cover any rings people cannot remove.)

- Demonstrate drumming technique. Emphasize the bouncing feeling when playing the drum. Like jumping on a trampoline or dribbling a basketball, people should be able to lightly bounce their hands off the drum.

- Hold your hand correctly. One common beginning drummer error is playing from the wrist. Hold up a mallet and then hold your forearm next to it, encouraging people to make a mallet with their hands and feel the pivot point at their elbows, not their wrist (with the exception of more subtle frame drum technique and slap and other more advanced sounds on djembes and congas).

- Hold the mallet correctly, not like a pencil or fork, but with a full hand wrapped grip. The mallet should also bounce off the drum to create proper technique.

- Hold the drum correctly. Demonstrate the importance of the bottom of the drum being raised off the ground for djembes to sound good.

- Noise management. Because everyone is sharing one sonic space there are key rules, such as *no banging on a bell next to someone else's ears*. Avoid being the noise police by cultivating an awareness of decibel level within the group.

Basic Hand Drumming Technique

The facilitator does not have to be a master drum teacher, but he/she does need to know the basic tones of hand drumming. It's most important to have a well-developed sense of rhythmicity. Rhythmicity is the natural instinct that causes your foot to land on the beat while you do aerobics or dance to your favorite music. When you don't step to the beat, something feels OFF. Cultivate rhythmicity in your personal musical expression and in your facilitating, and your circles will be a success.

Practice making a clear difference between the bass and tone on your drum.

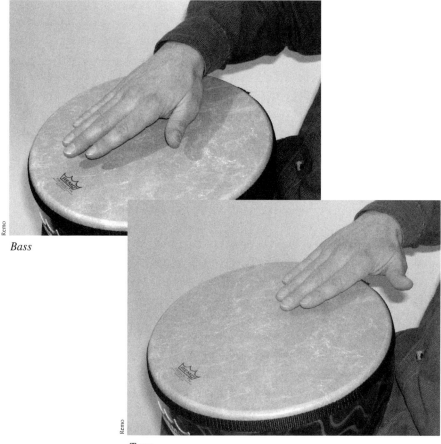

Bass

Tone

For more advanced drum tones, you can develop the slap sound by angling your hand on the edge of the drum to hear a high pitched pop sound. Check out any number of wonderful resources on the market specific to developing your personal hand drumming skills!

There are four main sounds on the drums that correlate with the four elements of earth, air, fire, and water:

- *Earth* – Bounce hand in center of drum for bass sound.

- *Air* – Brush the drum with open hand.

- *Fire* – Tap the rim or edge of drum head for tone or slap sound.

- *Water* – Leave hand on drum for a muffled closed bass sound.

See also: *The Healing Drum Learning Program*, Sounds True, Stevens (2016).

See also: YouTube Video Tutorial: https://youtu.be/b6UOFw5jNyk.

Five Methods of Teaching without Teaching

Our research at the Remo Recreational Music Center in North Hollywood taught us that people preferred to have some type of "lesson" for about 20 percent of the time, while the majority of the time (80 percent) they preferred recreational drumming...something we refer to as the Law of 80/20. Here are five methods of weaving teaching into the drum circle without creating performance anxiety for the beginning recreational drummers.

1. *Call and Response*—This is an amazing way to demonstrate key elements including:
   a. Rhythmic patterns
   b. Different vocal pitches of the drum
   c. Nontraditional sounds like rubbing the drumhead
   d. Dynamics

   AUDIO TRACK 5

2. *Metaphoric Teaching*—Using metaphors, you can create a fun way to demonstrate drumming techniques. For example, I've adapted a metaphoric system of teaching frame drum, created by Nubian composer Hamzin El Din, using the symbolism of the five elements:
   a. *Earth*—Open Bass (hand bounces in center of drum)
   b. *Fire*—Tone (hand bounces on edge of drum)
   c. *Water*—Closed Bass (hand lands in center of drum and stays on drum, like a drop of rain landing on the earth, getting soaked up)

    d. *Air*—Rubbing the Drum (rubbing the drumhead with hands, fingers, nails—fast or slow)

    e. Spirit—Silence (resting)

3. *Say It-Play It*—Many great drum teachers of varying traditions, from Glen Velez (Dum, Tak, Kah) to Babatunde Olatunji, (Goon, Doon, Go, Da, Pa, Ta), use the oral tradition of cultural drum instruction. By having their students speak and sing the language of the drums, they teach patterns and various tones. Before they even touch a drum, people have embodied the patterns and sounds of the drum, making them immediately successful when they play. You can use any verbal phrase or even someone's name to develop rhythmic patterns. After all, language is rhythmical.

4. *Passing Out Parts*—In the drum circle, simple rhythmic patterns come alive when put together with complementary patterns. By teaching and demonstrating parts to play, a group has an immediate experience in success. Watch the group to know when it's time to change the music and get back to making up their own parts.

5. *Games*—There's nothing like a game to remind people to *play*. For example, you can demonstrate bass tone within the context of Simon Says or Follow the Leader.

The Facilitator's Credo

As you join the facilitator community, you must solemnly swear to avoid these common pitfalls associated with teaching and performing.

I will not use exclusionary terms

Terms such as "real" drummers or "real" musicians make recreational players feel unworthy.

I will not judge success by the musical quality

Instead, pay attention to the number of smiles and laughs, and the faces of the people in the drum circle.

I will not treat the group as an "audience"

It's a trick to get used to being in the circle and spinning around as you work with the group, but it is important not to get in the habit of facing only one section, as if they are your audience.

I will not show off
Your amazing playing may actually intimidate recreational players. Use your talents whenever it's appropriate to support the circle's self-expression and fun.

I will not take all the credit
It's easy to be seen as the one responsible for all the incredible magic of the drum circle. A hungry ego will enjoy this stardom, however, the true credit belongs to the circle. As you acknowledge them, you give a lasting gift of confidence and a desire to keep playing.

Rules to Groove By

"Life has a flow, a rhythm, a groove. When we find our groove, it expresses itself in our daily activities, from simple to complex, from music to life." —Sammy K.,
Grammy-Nominated and Remo-Endorsed
Drummer and Drum Circle Facilitator

Groove—(*noun*) top form ("in the *groove*"). A pronounced enjoyable rhythm. (Merriam-Webster.com)

The goal of the groove is creating a pocket, the place where things "lock in." You feel the pocket in music when your playing becomes effortless and seems to be carried by the whole group. The one thing that can get in the way of the pocket is over-thinking. Grooving requires letting go and *feeling* more than *thinking*. The groove is always a destination for the drum circle, and it often is the moment that people feel the deepest connection.

Rules to Groove By

Here are some key principles to follow when getting the rhythm started.

1. Develop your personal groove first

It is important that you have a personal connection with the rhythm within you and the ability to improvise and express that rhythm on a percussion instrument. **AUDIO TRACKS 1, 2, 3**

2. Develop your groove repertoire

Be prepared with a good duple-meter groove. Playing in 2/4 or 4/4 is easiest for new drummers because it's like the rhythm of walking. We've been practicing it in our bodies for a long time. **AUDIO TRACK 1**

3. Don't be afraid of 6/8

From "London Bridge" to "Itsy Bitsy Spider," many of our favorite children's songs are in triple meter (3/4, 6/8, 12/8). Many modern-dance classes move in 6/8 because triple-meter grooves make you feel like swaying. This meter also holds the tempo, resisting the typical speeding up that happens in 4/4 or duple grooves. **AUDIO TRACK 2**

4. Put the needle on the record

Have a CD of world music with a driving rhythm playing as people arrive. They will naturally play along with the pre-established rhythmic groove, until they drown out the recording. Particularly with smaller groups, the CD provides anonymity for new drummers. **AUDIO TRACKS 1, 2, 3**

5. Sing them to the groove

Whether using your voice or a melodic instrument, a commonly-known song can create an immediate groove. Some songs to try…

"I'm Gonna Tell You How It's Gonna Be" (Followed by clave pattern.)

"Joy to the World" (Starts with "Jeremiah was a bullfrog," they play the rhythmic accents.)

"The Lion Sleeps Tonight" (Get ready to go to 6/8! You may even get spontaneous jungle and animal sounds.)

6. Start with a pulse, or pattern

Just playing a straight four creates an American Indian-sounding rhythm and is also a nice simple way for everyone to lock into a simple, basic pulse. To take it a step further, use a pulse variation that's more syncopated. A one-measure syncopated phrase can make a pattern, which is easily layered upon.

AUDIO TRACKS 1, 2, and 7 *begin with a straight pulse.* **AUDIO TRACKS 3 and 6** *begin with a pattern)*

7. Play the lyrics on the drum

A key method of starting a groove in long-term care centers is to have everyone play the words to a familiar song on their drums. For example, "I've been working on the railroad" makes a cool rhythmic pattern they can repeat, creating an ostinato.

8. The Heartbeat

Many people enjoy using the heartbeat rhythm, spoken as "lub dub, lub dub." This rhythm can go into 3/4 by leaving only one beat of space (lub dub rest/lub dub rest) or 4/4 by leaving two beats of space (lub dub rest rest/lub dub rest rest). Barry Bittman, MD actually uses a heart monitor connected to amplification to highlight the inherent rhythm in someone's heartbeat. After letting everyone listen, he cues the group to jam to that person's heartbeat rhythm.

Groove Management

Helping a group find the pocket is an ongoing job. Even after you get a good beat going, there can be challenges in keeping it together. Here are some tips for keeping the music going strong:

Assign a few people to the backbeat—i.e. shaker, tambourine, shakere.

Strengthen the pulse and add more emphasis to the ONE.

Stop for four counts and come back in. This always causes people to FEEL the rhythm inside and immediately the groove will improve when they play again.

Bring the volume down so everyone can listen to each other. Playing soft always helps solidify the groove.

Close their eyes—helping people relax encourages entrainment.

Say it to play it—use language, phrases like "uh-huh," to help line up the groove.

Clapping to the groove—keep the bass drum going and have everyone else clap on two and four.

Change the groove—sometimes a groove just isn't working. Know when to go in and end it in order to start a more successful new groove on the bass drum.

Groove Wreckers

Even then, there may be key distracters to the drum circle experience. These groove wreckers are your responsibility to redirect and engage in the awareness of the whole group experience. The drum circle is about creative freedom, and so many facilitators take on an attitude of letting whatever happens happen. I disagree. My rule of thumb is watching the whole group and taking the totality of the response into consideration. When one person is distracting or upsetting the majority of the group, you've got to intervene. How? Think of it like Judo. Instead of pushing hard against this force, find ways to allow it to take on a new role and shape in the drum circle.

Groove Wreckers	Management Strategies
Show-offs	Give them their moment to shine, applaud them, and offer them a new important survival role, like a bass drum. They CAN be your key rhythm allies or your worst nightmare.
Oblivious, "heads-down" drummers	Instead of singling them out, ask everyone in the drum circle to practice "heads-up" drumming and look across the circle to play to someone else.
Loud instruments	Offer softer mallets instead of sticks to quiet the sound.
Constant speeding up	Set the speed limit. The facilitator holds the Speed Limit Sign—watch your group and determine their maximum speed without leaving people out. Emphasize togetherness more than playing fast.
Out-of-control kids	This can seriously wreck the whole experience for some people. Kids are a blessing at a drum circle, but they require more structure. Remind parents to keep an eye on their children. The drum circle is not a babysitting program.

I've Got a Question

What do you do with the people who don't have rhythm? While I don't believe there is anyone who does not have rhythm, I do believe there are people who have been out of touch with their innate rhythm. They haven't been dancing, moving, drumming, and sometimes living! If you see someone struggling with the rhythm (usually indicated by a squished brow or playing loudly out of time), try…

- Offering an ambient instrument so they can play without the stress of following the beat.

- Offering an opportunity to put down their drum, close their eyes, and just feel the rhythm.

- Placing their hands on the drum to feel the vibration of the whole group.

- Offering an opportunity to move to the beat, in their seat or getting up and dancing.

- Moving them near the bass drum or moving the bass drum to them.

- Don't single them out! Be invisible with the way you assist them. Instead of correcting one individual, invite everyone to try these interventions.

- Sit next to them and play a similar drum very simply.

- Point out someone across the circle for them to follow.

Designing Your Program

"For me, drum circles are like going to church and a night on the town, rolled into one." —Kenneth Moore, Post Production Technician

Design—(*verb*) from *designare*, to outline, mean. To devise for a specific function or end. (Merriam-Webster.com)

While you can never predict the events within the drum circle, it's useful to have an overall plan, a map that includes a destination and a preferred route of travel. In fact, the drum circle is an *emergent ritual*, an in-the-moment experience of purpose that evolves and becomes clear along the way. The facilitator must always be open to changing directions and paying attention for clues of the group's experience.

Planning is a variable trait. Some people love *winging it*, while others approach life with a structured schedule and itinerary. Recognize your personal bias. If you are a planner, feel free to bring notes, outlines, games, and activities to your drum circle. In fact, kid's drum circles thrive on having structured games. Despite all your plans, the improvisational nature of drum circles will demand that you have the flexibility to change directions accordingly. Take a moment to think about your personal comfort zone. Rate yourself on this scale from 1 – 10:

1	2	3	4	5	6	7	8	9	10

Planner   *Spontaneous*

Four Tips in Designing Your Program

1. Know your audience

Go into the drum circle knowing as much as you can about the people you are working with and what they want to achieve. If you don't know, ask a few questions at the beginning, like "how many people are at a drum circle for the first time?"

2. Know your purpose

If the group is there for stress reduction, design a program that keeps them laughing. If the group is there for a spiritual experience, have a good song or chant ready to share. If the group is there for empowerment, consider a segment where you invite people from the group to facilitate.

3. Consider the group size

There are some great drum circle games that work better in smaller, more intimate circles. Yet, in smaller groups, people have less anonymity. I prefer to work with a minimum of fifteen people. In larger groups, you may want to add more space and quiet to balance the noise level.

4. Pace the program

The typical drum circle is one to two hours long, but some may be specifically thirty minutes. A common mistake is to run through all your "tricks" in the first fifteen minutes. Pace yourself. Once in a while, simply join the group and enjoy the jam.

Exercise: Draw a Picture

This idea was born out of dialogues between Stephanie Buffington and I after one of her amazing Pasadena drum circles. After your drum circle, sit down and draw yourself a picture, using a line. Draw a map, like an EKG that peaks and flows along time representing the total drum circle. Indicate places where you stopped and talked. This is a visual image of the overall program. Look at the highlights and see whether you were able to pace the group successfully.

Sample Format

There are a few key elements to weave into your drum circle program. At the Remo Recreational Music Center, we have created an outline, like a liturgy at a church service, that generally includes the following key elements:

10 min.   *Warm Up*—There is music playing as people arrive. They choose their drum and play along with the recording until a strong groove is established. Then we secretly fade out the music.

2 min.   *Welcome*—Welcome everyone, particularly people who are new.

2 min.   *Purpose statement*—A key opportunity to explain the philosophy of recreational drumming and the role of the facilitator in the drum circle.

2 min.   *Rules*—Ask the group to give me a big rumble if they can agree to each of these rules for the evening.

- Parents agree to be responsible for their own children.
- Drummers agree to remove their rings if hand drumming.
- Everyone agrees to be aware of keeping the volume level manageable.
- Everyone agrees to have fun.

Stretching out

3 min.	*Stretching*—An important step in preparing for the physical exercise of drumming and the use of the upper body muscles. Invite people to take a few deep breaths, gently stretch their wrists and forearms, tense and relax their shoulders and necks.
5 min.	*Drumming lesson*—A fun, brief review of proper technique.
40 min.	*Drum circle*—Using games and facilitation cues and arrangements, the group is now off to their rhythmical destination....the pocket.
2 min.	*Announcements and appreciations*—thank everyone who helped set up, greet people, or played a special part in the drumming.
5 min.	*Closing*—Whether it's a song or just taking time to breathe and stretch, the group needs a sense of closure and grounding before leaving the circle.

Body Beat™

Icebreaker Essentials

If you have many new people, it's a good idea to add an icebreaker to your program design. The best icebreakers for drum circles are ones that warm up the group while warming up the groove. Sammy K and I invented an icebreaker game called *Body Beat*™. Made up of thirty-four cards in a deck, they contain five key body-percussion sounds in cool complementary patterns; tap, lap, whap, clap, and snap (available at www.ubdrumcircles.com). Whether you use a non-drumming team-building game or a drum game like playing name rhythms, the key is to get a group to laugh and get comfortable with one another.

Drum Circle Games

Name Game—Probably the most famous and useful game is playing your name on the drums. It can be done in call and response, or to start a groove.

Call and Response Pass Off—You start a call and response pattern, and after the group has made their response, you choose the next person to be the leader. They in turn choose the next leader until everyone has a turn.

Sound Shape Twister—Using a Twister board and only the green, yellow, blue, and red sound shapes, choose someone to spin the dial. Have everyone play the drum of the color with their left or right hand, left or right foot.

Simon Says—Use Simon Says to call out rhythms or things like "Simon Says play the drum two times." "Simon Says play the drum with your elbows." Invite a few new Simon leaders into the middle to get everyone laughing.

Celebration Circle—This is an excellent ending game. Invite the group to rumble until someone comes into the center and facilitates a stop cut. That person says one thing they're celebrating and we're back to another rumble, waiting for the next person to recognize their personal cause to celebrate.

Tips for Working with Kids

In kids drum circles, a few extra rules and tools are important.

Mallets Up—It's so important to stop before you start. Teach kids the way to stop all together by cueing "mallets up" to indicate putting their mallets or hands up in the air.

Whistle Stop—It's a gym class thing. When kids hear a whistle they naturally freeze. I use a samba whistle as a cueing agent.

Pace the Instruments—Thanks to Bob Bloom and Cameron Tummel, I've learned not to start with every instrument available. By starting with body percussion, adding shakers,

Max and Caden Stevens with Aunt Christine

then adding drums without mallets, then mallets, you create a natural excitement to hold kid's attention and keep them engaged.

Stories and Imagination—Instead of a mallet or beater for their sound shapes, I tell kids it's a *magic wand*, and if they all stop together and point their wands to heaven, all our wishes will come true.

Separate Boys and Girls—Seriously. If you're working with middle-school kids, hormones will get in the way of your best efforts. I tell the kids that in ancient times, the men and women met in separate circles, so let's do that today.

Closing the Circle

I often end with a song, a poem, or a question, "Does anyone have anything they want to say about this experience tonight?" The facilitator doesn't have all the answers. Ask if anyone has a song or poem to share. You'll be surprised. Without this step, I've had scary reports of people getting lost while driving home because they feel un-grounded. Here is a sample ending that helps to ground the participants at the end of the circle.

Exercise: Closing the Circle

Invite the group to take a few deep breaths. Ask them to place their feet on the ground and to feel the floor below their feet. Invite them to close their eyes and place their hands on their instrument. Invite them to offer gratitude and thanks to the drum, for its rhythm and song, and its reflection of the rhythm within them. When they are ready, ask them to open their eyes and look around the circle, offering the same gratitude without speaking, to all the people who came to drum with them. Encourage them to take the rhythm with them as they leave.

The ending is sometimes the beginning. Keep reading and discover a deeper side of the drum circle and the methodology to facilitate personal change and transformation along with the song in the drum circle.

II

The HEART of Drum Circles

Helene Barbara

"Drumming provides a quick and easy access to musical conversation. Talia and I can be an integral part of the musical dialogue." —Michael Blare, Carpenter

"Drumming is like a way to express yourself in something you're good at." —Talia Blare, student

Inseparable Elements

Although this book addresses the art and the heart as separate sections, they are interdependent. Simply put; the art is not apart from the heart of the drum circle. (Say that three times fast!) There can be a heartfelt connection that is built through the music that is just as strong a foundation as the rhythmical pulse that entrains the group. In this perspective, your job as a facilitator expands beyond the music and into the potential to bring out the best in all people.

Whole Person Perspective

The term "whole person" refers to the holistic perspective of body, mind, and spirit. Music making is probably one of the oldest mind-body-spirit techniques making a comeback in mainstream health and wellness movements today. Whereas a music teacher must focus primarily on technique and performance, the drum circle facilitator must focus on much more than the music, including the personality, caring, support, and key human elements of the drum circle.

Purpose

There are many reasons why people attend drum circles that have nothing to do with music. These non-musical outcomes create the framework for your facilitation techniques and way of conducting the drum circle. Consider this list of benefits of recreational drumming. Keep adding to the list as you witness people's experiences in your drum circle.

- Fun
- Self-expression
- Stress reduction
- Unity
- Community building
- Exercise for mind, body, and spirit
- Camaraderie and support
- Multi-generational family connection
- Spiritual experience

Drum circles offer much more than the music. They offer the opportunity to reconnect with the heart, to be playful, and to practice support and appreciating each other's song. In fact, focusing too much on the music can blind you to the young teenager in the last row who spontaneously offers to hold the drum for the older woman sitting next to him. This section invites you to view the success of the drum circle within the context of the human experience, and to consider the methods of facilitation that best support achieving these goals.

Transformation

Drumming in community brings you from your head into your heart, where joy lives and transformation begins."
— Stephanie Buffington, Drum Circle Facilitator

Transformation—(*noun*) moving beyond one's perceived limitations. (Merriam-Webster.com)

Drum circles have the potential to touch people's lives beyond the music in a powerful way. In asking people about their experience in the drum circle, the word transformational is often heard. The word transformation literally indicates moving beyond the "form" of the drum circle. People's lives can be enhanced and even profoundly changed through two key elements of the drum circle; the self-expression and community connection. This transformation can be a holistic experience on all three levels; body, mind, and spirit.

1. *Body*—discovery of physical capabilities that were hidden or forgotten. It's the person who uses their cane to walk to the drum circle, but somehow gets up and dances without it. It's the person who has never drummed before, but whose hands intuitively feel a connection to the drum and naturally begin to play. It's my friend Heather MacTavish, who, despite Parkinson's, not only drums, but also facilitates drum circles in long-term care centers. It's moving beyond any physical barrier that people thought would stop them from drumming, proving to themselves that it is achievable.

2. *Mind*—discovery of new focus and truth. The opportunity to turn off the busy mind, and to overcome negative thoughts and self-limiting beliefs. It's the person who was told they don't have rhythm who has the courage to come to the drum circle and discover that they can feel the rhythm and naturally follow the beat. It's the person who tries unsuccessfully to meditate who finds that drumming takes their mind off their problems.

3. *Spirit*—discovery of connection and unity—discovery of Spirit. It's the person who feels alone and struggles to reach out to others who spontaneously hugs a complete stranger at the end of the drum circle. It's the person who doesn't believe in God but who somehow finds the feeling of spirituality for the first time in the drum circle. Through the support and love of community, people can make remarkable strides beyond the challenges of their life.

Don't think for one second that this level of transformation is reserved for enlightened adults. This poem was written by a twelve-year-old boy who attends the community drum circle every Tuesday night at the Remo Recreational Music Center in North Hollywood, California.

Helene Barbara

When I Drum
By Sean Scheuering, age 12

When I drum I can hear my heart beat
I feel excitement from my head to my feet
It takes away my pain and worry
I don't feel like I'm in such a hurry.

When I am drumming I feel free
My troubles fly away from me
And in comes all the peace and love
My spirit soars just like a dove.

When I am drumming with my friends
I feel like we are family
And when we drum we sound like one
One heart, one soul, one mind.

The Essential 3 x 5 Cards

Although you can always just ask people from your drum circle to share their experience, you might consider this practice to keep growing in your understanding of the deeper impact of the drum circle. Allowing people to anonymously write it down will generate more honest responses, and it also gives the group an opportunity to reflect on the experience and let it sink in.

Exercise: Getting Feedback

Bring a stack of 3 x 5 cards and pens/pencils to your drum circle. Ask everyone to write one sentence about their experience in the drum circle on the card, anonymously. As people write, they reflect on the drum circle and translate their unique personal experience into words. It provides them with a reflective tool and provides you with important information on what the drum circle is really about. It can be incredibly moving. These quotes are also useful endorsements for your drum circle flyers and brochures.

The Heart of Facilitation

"Drum circles help Japanese express themselves in a non-verbal form and allow them to connect, support and empower themselves through rhythm." —Tomoko Yokota,
Co-Founder Orange Boom Boom

Heart—(*noun*) one's innermost character, feelings, or inclinations. (Merriam-Webster.com)

Heart-based facilitation deals with who you are and carrying your authentic presence into the circle. It is the way you show the group that you care. The drum circle is like a giant mirror. Whatever you give will be reflected back to you 100 times stronger. When you go into the drum circle worried that you're going to make a mistake, the group will seem nervous and unsettled. But when you offer your joy and your heart, it will come back to you multiplied and magnified.

Personal Preparation

Before the beat begins, take some time to prepare yourself. Prepare your body through stretching and breathing. Remember that facilitation can really be a workout. Take some deep breaths to relax and clear your mind as well. Before you start the drum circle, take a moment to try the following focusing technique to re-inspire yourself through remembering your musical joy.

Exercise: Anchoring Yourself in Musical Joy

Take a moment to reflect on your first joyous musical experience. How old were you? Who was there with you? Where were you and what were you doing? Do you remember the feeling, the connection with music, and the people you were with? Sing, hum, or dance the music you associate with this memory.

Just as the anchor is a boat's connection to the deepest place in the ocean, use this memory and feeling as the base of your facilitation. Anchor yourself in this positive musical place, and you will inspire the musical joy of others in your drum circle.

Skills of the Heart

There are skills or qualities that may have been previously considered outside of the realm of the tools for facilitating the drum circle. Within this perspective, the facilitator is now open to sharing themselves with the circle in a whole new way and drawing upon their personal qualities and experience. Often people feel unqualified to facilitate drum circles because they are not master drummers. Understanding that the facilitation is equally heart-based reminds us that there are skills and qualities of who we are and what we've experienced in our lives that now directly apply. From coaching soccer to leading a work task force, your facilitation of non-musical activities now directly applies. Whether you study the great coaches or great leaders, the key is always caring about the people and empowering them to discover and share the gifts within themselves.

Here is a beginning list of heart skills to cultivate in your facilitation:

Courage—being brave enough to come into the center of the circle and "stand in the fire."

Authenticity—being yourself.

Rapport—building the connection and trust.

Charisma—generating enthusiasm.

Caring—sharing and showing your support.

Humor—laughing at life and at yourself.

Seeing—looking with your eyes and listening with your heart to what the group needs.

Positive attitude—recognizing that there are no mistakes, only opportunities to learn.

Flexibility—happily being spontaneous with changes that emerge.

Intention

Remember entrainment, the power of synchronization between two rhythms? Intention can also create an entrainment effect, particularly when the facilitator comes to the circle with a clear and strong focus on what the group can attain and accomplish. When you begin with the end in mind, you generate a current of positive flow that can bring all other thoughts in line with it.

Check in with your heart to see what your intention is for your drum circle. It may be simply to help people let go, or to help the quieter people have a voice in the community. It may be as intense as reconnecting after a tragedy such as September 11 or the Columbine High School shooting. Think outside of the music and tune in to the purpose of the drum circle each time you facilitate. As you embody the purpose of the drum circle in your heart, it will be reflected back to you and serve to inspire the people who think they have come just to drum, but leave with much more than the rhythm.

Play

There is a reason we say that we *play* music. There is a hidden playfulness in every grown-up, that child within that used to bang on the pots and pans in the kitchen. To empower the playfulness of your drum circles, try using trickery, sneakiness, and other crafty ideas that inspire a group to laugh while drumming. Laughter opens the heart and frees the spirit. That is why general foolishness and silliness are wonderful things to bring into the drum circle. The sound of every drummer in the circle laughing out loud is the best song you can get a group to *play*.

The REAL Instruments

David Rumley

"The children I work with at the Center love to drum. The drum circle gives them the chance to express themselves and opens the door to communicate with each other in a safe environment."
—Sundiata Kata,
Director of Music and Performing Arts,
San Diego Center for Children

Real Instruments—(*noun*) human beings, born with an innate ability to create sound and move rhythmically; *homo-musicalis*.

Human beings are naturally musical. We are all born with two biological instruments; our voice and the rhythm within our hearts. Music is everyone's birthright. Rhythm is a particularly biological element. We are all walking, talking, ticking, tocking polyrhythms.

Music is America's favorite past time, and yet, so many people have stopped making music in their lives. The drum circle is the antidote to the suppression of our musical voice. It gives people a tool to say what words cannot express, to speak from the heart through the musical mirror the drum provides.

Drum Circle Fear

Musicians and drummers take for granted the ease they have in approaching instruments. But some people are incredibly intimidated by music. In fact, some people who come to the drum circle have inherited so many myths about music making, they can't have any fun at it. They believe the lies that you had to have some great remarkable talent or you weren't musical. The lies that some people had rhythm and others did not. I've learned many key insights by talking with the people who had a negative experience at my drum circles. From their perspective, there are four fears that can be barriers to their musical enjoyment.

1. Fear of performance

2. Fear of losing the beat

3. Fear of being put on the spot

4. Fear of looking stupid

Antidotes

Despite these fears, many people are still incredibly motivated by a longing to make music, and particularly to play a drum. There is a saying that "energy flows where attention goes." The facilitator can help dispel these fears by refocusing the attention from fear to belief, from performance to fun, and from what they can't do to what they can do. Secondly, the facilitator creates a safe atmosphere that emphasizes creativity and exploration rather than right or wrong. Here is my list of the top ten facilitation tips and tricks to destroy drum circle fears:

1. *Laughing*—Trickery that cracks up a group, a good joke, and a fun game is key. The shave and a haircut rhythm always gets the "two bits" response and cracks up a group. This is a signature Arthur Hull move that he often uses to end a jam.

2. *Beauty in numbers*—Don't isolate one person or a few people who are new at this! This type of drum circle trauma will reduce the number of people who return next time.

3. *Close your eyes*—Darkening a room or asking everyone to close their eyes can be very important in developing safety and reducing fear of looking stupid. When you tune out, you tune in.

4. *Play to someone else*—Ask the group to choose someone across the circle to connect with while playing.

5. *Play like someone else*—There are many teachers in the drum circle. Invite people to steal a pattern from anyone else in the circle at any moment. This keeps a group connected and paying more attention to each other, and less attention to the facilitator.

6. *Play on someone else's drum*—Asking the group to play each other's drums helps them literally reach out to one another and quells the fear of standing out.

7. *Icebreakers*—Any crazy game that helps people laugh and get to know one another has a place in building the camaraderie and connection that will help put people at ease.

8. *Soundscapes*—There's no fear of losing the beat when you're using ambient instruments and soundscapes.

9. *Take a deep breath*—Relaxation is key. Remind people to relax their shoulders and take a few deep breaths. Because drums are NOT a breath instrument, it is important to remind people to breathe while playing.

10. *Facilitator mistakes*—YES, I'm suggesting that the facilitator shouldn't always be perfect. It's important to be humble and make mistakes in front of your circle.

Using Your Voice

Why is singing important? After all, this is a drum circle, not a choir.

When people use their voice, it activates the whole-person musicality that is the biological inheritance of all people. When they're just drumming, people sometimes have the sense that the music is just in their hands. Bringing in the voice, whether through singing, chanting, toning, or vocalizing, causes people to suddenly be more animated as they rediscover the most innate musical gift, their voice. However, singing has its own unique barriers to overcome. Many people have been told, "you can't carry a tune in a bucket." Your job is to dump out the bucket.

In tribal culture, drum circles often include singing. It is a powerful method of group bonding. When people sing together, they breathe together. The shift of bringing in the voice happens by the facilitator being willing to use their own voice first. Be courageous and experiment in your drum circles with friends. Sing in the shower. When you're ready to weave vocals into the drum circle, try some of these facilitation tips:

- Bring a song to the circle.

- Stop the drumming but keep the bass drum going and have people use one-syllable sounds to scat rhythmically and keep the groove going (la, da, de, da...).

- Improvise and vocalize on laughing syllables (ha ha ha ha ha).

- Try call and response with voice.

- Start by singing one note on "la" and ask everyone to harmonize.

- Try a guttural "huh" placed on the fourth beat of any measure, to create the old-school funk "thang."

- "Bop Whop a Loo Bop, A Whap Bam Boom." Try using the shave and a haircut of vocal jamming in a call and response format with the drum circle.

Talking in Circles

"Drumming is the language that joins hearts and opens forgotten reasons to live. To drum is to speak without words and truly listen."
—Dr. Larry Graber, PhD

Talking—(*verb*) to influence, affect, or cause by conversing or communicating.

Recreational drumming is as much a mind-set as it is a practice. Using your words in the drum circle helps maintain this perspective and makes the transfer of the drum circle experience into everyday life. This mind-set emphasizes being playful, creative, expressive, and connecting to one's community; elements that certainly benefit our lives, even after the rhythm of the drum circle stops.

Because group drumming creates a heightened sense of openness and an awareness of the present moment, people will remember what you say long after the drum circle ends. They may surprisingly forget a rhythm they've played for over thirty minutes, but somehow remember the two sentences you said right after the whole group stopped together in perfect silence. I've had people remind me at least one year after a drum circle of something I said that had great meaning to them. So use your words wisely and recognize the power of what you say. Offer the group in words the message you'd like to have echo in their lives and resonate in their hearts.

Timing is important. There is often a beautiful silence that occurs at the end of a piece in the drum circle. Let the silence sit for a moment before taking these opportunities to affirm the positive and emphasize the potential for transformation. Be a positive mirror, reflecting back all the good things you are seeing, hearing, and sensing.

In the excellent book, *The Way of Council* (Zimmerman, Coyle, 1996), there are four rules that are helpful in considering the heart of the message. Derived from the indigenous tribal practice of gathering a council of leaders and elders to dialogue about key issues and make decisions for tribal life, this approach is being used in today's schools and communities...and drum circles.

1. *Speak from the heart.* Use creative communication and share your feelings.

2. *Listen from the heart.* Let your heart be open to the magic of the drum circle.

3. *Speak leanly.* Keep your comments brief and powerful.

4. *Don't rehearse.* Be in the moment. Catch the group doing something amazing and reflect it back to them.

Being Heard

Obviously, the drum circle is often a loud art form. If you want to speak, make sure you can be heard. Asking people to be quiet and listen is a win-win proposition. They get a break from drumming and a moment of reflection to allow the experience to sink into their psyche.

Reflecting and Sharing

There are many ways in which the facilitator uses their words to convey the message and meaning of the drum circle. Here is a list to get you thinking about what you'd like to say.

Welcome and congratulate new drummers and newcomers—Everyone's first drum circle is pretty memorable. Honor and recognize this special experience for all new participants.

Make a homework assignment—By saying things like "tonight take a moment to write in your journal about the lessons and feelings you discovered during this drum circle. Share your experience with someone close to you and see how you describe it."

Speak in the affirmative—Be a positive mirror, a reflection of the best of the drum circle experience.

Offer gratitude—Thank all the people who helped to make the drum circle happen. Thank the ancestors. Thank all the participants. Thank the bass drum players. Be thankful and full of gratitude. It's a great way to help the circle be appreciative of all it offers.

Say less to say more—We are all in love with our own voice. Be careful not to go on and on. Make your speech brief and it will carry more power.

Make the transfer—If drumming is not just about drumming, how will people reflect on what it is truly about unless you assist them in driving home the point of how the drum circle experience can transfer into their lives, even when they're not sitting in front of their drum. Because rhythm is everywhere, it's an easy transfer to make.

Plant seeds—By saying things like "this experience will change you. Even tomorrow you may notice a certain bounce to your step that feels like a rhythm."

Use a metaphor—By saying things like, "For me, this drum circle is a multi-colored mosaic of all the rhythms we're sharing tonight," you invite many different perspectives on what the drum circle meant and symbolized to each person.

Pop the Question

When you ask a question to the drum circle, you offer them an opportunity to reflect upon their experience and listen to others' reflections, which sometimes perfectly describe their own experience.

There are many formats used when asking a group question. You can invite people to raise their hands to answer, or invent creative ways, such as inviting everyone to share their response with someone sitting near them in the circle. You can even invite ambient instruments to play background music while people stand and share.

Pay attention to the type of question you ask—varying from open-ended to quite specific yes/no types. Encourage the group to speak from their hearts. And don't think for a second that kids can't do this—they often have the most profound answers to the deepest questions!

Here are a few great questions to start you in generating your own list:

- Do you feel different than when you first arrived?

- What are you taking from tonight's experience?

- What are you letting go of? (I actually have people tip their drums over and look inside before I ask this question.)

- What just happened? (a great standard question for any time an amazing surprise occurs)

- Whose spirit inspired you tonight?

- What's one thing about tonight that you want to take into tomorrow?

Exercise: One Word

At the close of the drum circle, ask people to think of one word to describe their experience. Starting a soft pulse with only the facilitator playing, ask the group to go around the circle and one-by-one share their word on the beat. This creates a song poem of the experiences of the drum circle participants.

Metaphor

"How we play and interact when drumming reflects how we approach life; as such, drumming can offer a unique opportunity for self-discovery, connection, and empowerment."

—Ping Ho, MA, MPH,
Founder and Director of UCLArts and Healing

Metaphor—(*noun*) from Latin *metaphora*, to transfer. A word or phrase literally denoting one kind of object or idea used in place of another to suggest a likeness or analogy between them. (Merriam-Webster.com)

Metaphor is the methodology of transferring the meaning of the drum circle into life. Metaphor is memorable and illustrates universal principles of living in a language that often paints a clear and unforgettable picture. The metaphor lasts after the music ends.

It is the message of team building inherent in the drum circle that makes it a useful tool for corporations. It is the experience of a natural high that makes it important for recovering alcoholics. It is the practice of taking an active role in health and healing for a group of cancer survivors. It is the power of unity that makes it a powerful tool for diversity and multicultural education.

Musical language is already woven into many metaphoric sayings about life. From "living in perfect harmony," to "singing off on the same sheet of music," the connection of music to life is already apparent and strong. We just need to find the words to represent how the drum circle is an active, moving, dancing metaphor for life itself.

Forest for the Trees

Metaphor is all about perspective. With one sentence, you can help everyone see the drum circle as something completely different. Your metaphor can offer a change of perception and the integration of a purpose. In the words of Remo Belli, CEO/Owner, Remo, "It's time to stop thinking of the drum as just a musical instrument. Start thinking of it as a unifying tool for every family, a wellness tool for every retiree and an educational tool for every classroom."

For example, after the September 11th tragedy, we led the drum circle according to two key metaphors; reflection and rejuvenation. The music

Drum circle after 9-11 at Cal State Northridge

for the two sections was completely different. For the first section, based on an idea by music therapist Ron Borczon, we handed out the names of individuals killed from the state of California and asked people to drum their name rhythms. For the second section, we invited the group to drum their intentions for change in our world. We ended by inviting twelve people from different racial and religious groups to join together on the Remo drum table. They started the closing rhythm as a symbol and metaphor of unity and peace.

To develop your personal metaphor repertoire, try this exercise:

Exercise: Fill in the Blank
Without using any words related to drums or drumming, fill in the blanks with as many non-musical ideas as you can come up with.

The drum is LIKE _____

_____

The drum circle is LIKE _____

_____

Reflect on some amazing drum circle experiences of your own and consider what they really meant.

Universal Metaphors
Unity
There is a unique quality of togetherness that is experienced in the drum circle. We talk about "the one" in music. However, the metaphoric "one" has to do with the fact that we are all connected. The drum circle reminds us of this. It is an immediate experience in team building. If you don't see the drums, all you see is a group of people, all working together, expressing their unique voice in a group song, united by a common pulse. The drum circle is a metaphor for the best way people can connect and live in harmony.

Diversity
There are great differences between the people and sounds and rhythms shared in the drum circle. It is rich with diversity. Each person brings a unique spice to the flavor of the drum circle and should be acknowledged. The drum circle inherently honors diversity.

Life

The drum circle is a metaphor for a way of living that envelops sharing, expression, connection, creativity, and of course, playfulness.

Personal Metaphors

Each person enters the circle with their own gifts to offer and their own needs to fulfill. They have a unique way of seeing and understanding their experience. Someone may walk into the drum circle feeling discouraged and alone. By coincidence, the person next to them reaches out to show them the way to hold their drum. All of a sudden, they feel cared about and supported. That is because in this moment, the drum is no longer a drum. It is a gift, a symbol of support and connection just when they needed it.

The drum can represent infinite things, such as power, a voice, a tool, a gift, a mirror. Allow each person to ascribe the metaphor from their personal drum circle experience and create their own perspective for their own story.

Passing the Spark

For me, this book has been a metaphor. I am passing on much more than the knowledge and information of facilitating drum circles. I am passing on my passion and deep conviction that drum circles are a tool of social change. That is the true spark and torch I pass on to you. That is what the ancient tribes knew and practiced.

Just think of the many people who are now facilitating drum circles all over the world at this very moment. You now belong to this rapidly growing team, headed towards the finish line of providing musical access to all people.

I encourage you to offer the drum circle experience to as many people as you can, to be open to the calling for drum circles for various groups in your community and in your life, and to inspire all you come in contact with to reconnect to the rhythm within their hearts.

The more you share it, the stronger it grows within you.

Pick up the torch. Join the groove.

About the Audio

This audio really has three key purposes:

1. To develop your personal rhythmic skills and confidence by playing along with the tracks.

2. To jump-start your drum circle or to change the groove at any point, by inviting people to drum along to the audio.

3. Reflective Rehearsal—pop on the facilitation tracks and practice your body cues in the mirror.

TRACK 1 4/4 Groove

Tempo = 96   Duple meter

This 4/4 groove features a simple djun djun part and bell pattern, with nice conga and djembe parts inside. A strong bell pattern helps hold the rhythm together, while a tambourine on the backbeat spices up the mix. You can play along on bell, drums, or percussion, matching any of the patterns you hear, or making up your own pattern.

TRACK 2 6/8 Groove

Tempo = 108   Triple meter

This 6/8 groove features a strong djun djun part, cool bell pattern, shaker on the pulse, and middle drums. If you just listen, you'll hear some sweet dialogues between conga and djembe. Try moving to the music, and you'll discover why dancers tend to love this groove!

TRACK 3 Funk Groove

Tempo = 89   Duple meter

If you do any work with teens, this is a must – know rhythm and a useful track in starting up the drum circle. This 4/4 swung groove features bass drum, clap tracks, tambourine, conga, and djembe.

TRACK 4 Facilitated Drum Circle

Tempo = 105   Duple meter

A sample of a facilitated drum circle, this track is for you to practice your body language cues along with the verbal ones you hear. Don't be afraid to watch in a mirror. Facilitation is a visual job. I've broken down the road map of this piece to assist you in understanding and practicing what goes on.

1. Rumbles using dynamic swells until a beat emerges.

2. Counting to stop and start while varying the length of the stop and adding breathing into the stop. (In arrangement terms, this is a theme and variation.)

3. Dynamics are used in an arrangement of loud and soft.

4. Sculpting one player (bass drum) and weaving claps over the solo. Congas, djembe, shakers, and bells are sculpted next for solos (by showing the keep playing and then stopping the rest of the group).

5. Accents of one or two beats over the groove.

6. Speeding up—twice.

7. Big countdown to the end.

TRACK 5 Soundscape

Free tempo.

A great example of the use of ambient percussion sounds and a non-pulse based composition. This features spring drum, ocean drum, rain stick, chimes, and of course, drummers playing in a unique way to create a sonic poem. Dialogues between contrasting timbre groups (bass drum, shakers, bells) and style of playing (one beat versus rumbles) create an aesthetic arrangement. To book-end the piece, we feature a sweet chime at the opening and closing.

TRACK 6 Call and Response

Tempo = 95   Duple meter

A sample of call and response featuring djembe, conga, bass drum, and vocals leading the call and response, into a speed-up ending. A good example of beginning by counting in the groove.

▊TRACK 7▊ Melodic Facilitation

Tempo = 98   Duple meter

Begins by layering in djun djun, shaker, djembe, and conga. This track demonstrates bringing the volume of the drum circle down and adding a little flute melody over the groove. It is filled with arrangement strategies including melodic call and response, duets between flute and individual drummers (djembe and conga), and rhythmic accents supporting the melody (which I cued with my feet while playing the flute).

Many thanks to the drum circle players:

Cynthia Fitzpatrick

Christine Stevens

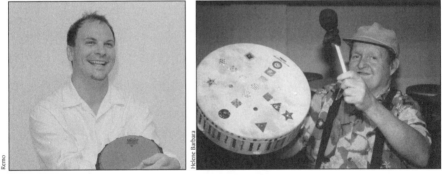

Sammy K   *James Patrick*

Cynthia Fitzpatrick: conga, ocean drum, shakers

Christine Stevens: shaker, tambourine, flute, rainstick, facilitation cues

Sammy K: bell, ashiko, djembe, tambourine, spring drum

James Patrick: djun djun, chimes

Recorded and mixed at El Oro Way Recording Studios.
All drums and world percussion instruments courtesy of Remo, Inc.

Resources for Further Information

Rhythm to Recovery: A Practical Guide to Using Rhythmic Music, Voice, and Movement for Social and Emotional Development
by Simon Faulkner

World Music Drumming: Across Cultural Curriculums
by Will Schmid

The Healing Power of the Drum
by Robert Lawrence Friedman

Drum Circle Spirit: Facilitating Human Potential through Rhythm
by Arthur Hull

When the Drummers Were Women: A Spiritual History of Rhythm
by Layne Redmond

Drumming at the Edge of Magic: A Journey into the Spirit of Percussion
by Mickey Hart

Planet Drum: A Celebration of Percussion and Rhythm
by Mickey Hart

Spirit into Sound: The Magic of Music
by Mickey Hart

The Drummer's Path:
Moving the Spirit with Ritual and Traditional Drumming
by Sule Greg C. Wilson

Ritual: Power, Healing, and Community
by Malidoma Patrice Some

The Healing Drum: African Wisdom Teachings
by Yaya Diallo

Music Medicine: The Science and Spirit of Healing Yourself with Sound
by Christine Stevens

Buffalo Woman Comes Singing:
The Spirit Song of a Rainbow Medicine Woman
by Brooke Medicine Eagle

Drum Circle: A Guide to World Percussion
by Chalo Eduardo and Frank Kumor

DRUM (Discipline, Respect, and Unity through Music)
by Jim Solomon

Videos

The Art and Heart of Drum Circles DVD
by Christine Stevens (Hal Leonard, 2005)
Watch a preview on YouTube: https://youtu.be/0bsBiRjgd2M/.

UpBeat Drum Circles YouTube Channel
https://www.youtube.com/user/ubdrumcircles

CDs
Available on iTunes and www.ubdrumcircles.com

Mickey Hart: At the Edge of Magic
  Supralingua

Babatunde Olatunji: Drums of Passion

Christine Stevens: The Healing Drum Learning Program
  2 CD set

Christine Stevens: DRUM! Reviving Rhythms, UpBeat Drum Circles

Christine Stevens: Drumming up DIVA—Women's
  Empowerment Drumming

Christine Stevens: Drumming up Spirit

Web Resources
Christine's personal website

UpBeat Drum Circles
www.ubdrumcircles.com

American Music Therapy Association (AMTA)
www.musictherapy.org

Remo Drum Company
www.remo.com

HealthRHYTHMS™
www.remo.com/experience/health-and-wellness/

DCFG Drum Circle Facilitators Guild
www.dcfg.net/

NAMM Foundation
www.nammfoundation.org

Village Music Circles
www.villagemusiccircles.com

Remo Drum Circle Finder
www.remo.com/experience/post/remo-rhythm-event-and-facilitator-finder/

Remo Drum Circle Resources
www.remo.com/experience/recreation/

About the Author

Bryan Leonard

Internationally acclaimed author, speaker, and music therapist Christine Stevens has trained thousands of facilitators from more than twenty-five countries in the evidence-based Remo HealthRHYTHMS™. Together with Navajo elder Manny Eagle Elk Council Pipe Sandoval, she created the Change Your Life Through RHYTHM facilitation training program, now available online. Featured on PBS, Discovery Channel, and in the DVD Discover the Gift, Christine has worked with Fortune 500 companies, survivors of Katrina, and students at Ground Zero. Together with an inspired team, Christine led the first drum circle training in a war-zone in northern Iraq.

Other works include the books *The Healing Drum Learning Program, Music Medicine*, and *Sound Shape Playbook*, as well as the DVD and streaming video *The Art and Heart of Drum Circles*.

UpBeat Drum Circles

We love to stay in touch with you!

Visit www.ubdrumcircles.com to learn more about training programs, retreats, and products to support your daily drum lifestyle. Sign up for the FREE monthly RDA: Recommended Drumming Allowance. Follow us on social media @ubdrumcircles.

Learn to lead drum circles with the Change Your Life Through RHYTHM online course available at www.ubdrumcircles.com/courses.

To learn more about Remo's HealthRHYTHMS™ and upcoming training programs, contact Remo via email at healthrhythms@remo.com. Visit us on the web at www.remo.com/experience/health-and-wellness/.

UpBeat Drum Circles

About Remo's Recreational Music Center
(RMC), Valencia, California

More than innovators in instrument development, Remo Inc. has been pioneering centers for recreational music making, known throughout the world as the Recreational Music Center, RMC. The center has received recognition from the California Senate, Congress, and County Board of Supervisors for "enriching the lives of others through music."

Ongoing research and program development at the center serves to inform the music industry of the best methods that broaden the scope of music makers and provide places where people can go to PLAY music. It was the dream of founder Remo Belli to duplicate the maiden RMC, which originated and operated in North Hollywood, California, under manager Mike DeMenno for over seventeen years. Now there are Remo RMC affiliates throughout the United States in places like Las Vegas, San Diego, Scottsdale, and Indianapolis. Learn more at http://remormc.com/.